ANGELS
AMONG US

A Testament of Divine Intervention That Will Transform Your Perspective

TRUDY FINNEY

DALLAS, TEXAS

All rights reserved. No part of this book may be reproduced or transmitted in any form or by any means, electronic or mechanical, including photocopying, recording, or by any information storage and retrieval system, without permission in writing from the copyright owner. The views expressed in this work are solely those of the author and do not necessarily reflect the views of the publisher, and the publisher hereby disclaims any responsibility for them.

Higgins Publishing. All rights reserved. *Angels Among Us: A Testament of Divine Intervention That Will Transform Your Perspective* © 2025 *

Higgins Publishing supports the rights to free expression and the value of copyright. The purpose of copyright is to encourage writers and artists to produce creative works that enrich our values.

The scanning, uploading, and distribution of this book without the express permission of the publisher is a theft of intellectual property. If you would like permission to use material from this book (other than for review purposes), please contact permissions@higginspublishing.com. Thank you for your support of copyright law.

Higgins Publishing | higginspublishing.com - The publisher is not responsible for websites (or their content) that are not owned by the publisher. Higgins Publishing is committed to excellence in the publishing industry. The company reflects the philosophy established by the founder, based on Psalm 68:11, The Lord gave the word, great was the company of those who proclaimed it (NKJV).

Scripture taken from the New King James Version®. Copyright © 1982 by Thomas Nelson, Inc. Used by permission. All rights reserved.

Library of Congress Control Number: 2025915110   December 2025
p.c.m. 116 * Includes Index

Finney, Trudy — *Angels Among Us: A Testament of Divine Intervention That Will Transform Your Perspective*

ISBN: 978-1-968931-00-1 (Paperback)
ISBN: 978-1-968931-01-8 (E-Book)

REL012040 RELIGION / Christian Living / Inspirational
REL012020 RELIGION / Christian Living / General
BIO018000 BIOGRAPHY & AUTOBIOGRAPHY / Religious
REL012110 RELIGION / Christian Living / Personal Memoirs
SEL032000 SELF-HELP / Spiritual
FAM009000 FAMILY & RELATIONSHIPS / Abuse / Domestic Partner Abuse

Our books may be purchased in bulk for promotional, educational, fundraising or business use. Please contact your local bookseller or Higgins Publishing Sales Department at, sales@higginspublishing.com.

First Edition: December 2025

Dedication

"For He will give His angels orders concerning you, to protect you in all your ways." Psalm 91:11

To the people I lovingly described in this testimony, I pray that God has touched your lives in some way. I thank you for being in my life at the right time and place that God determined you should be. Whether you knew it or not, you were obedient to God's instruction concerning me, and that is the reason I can share this testimony of God's faithfulness.

God bless you!

"Give thanks for everything to God the Father in the name of our Lord Jesus Christ." Ephesians 5:20

TABLE OF CONTENTS

FOREWORD I

INTRODUCTION III

Chapter One 1
My First Encounter with Angels: Crossing the Bridge

Chapter Two 17
God's Deliverance from Death: His Voice ....

Chapter Three 35
Road Trip Angel ....

Chapter Four 41
Hotel Angels ....

Chapter Five 71
Letter Attacks ....

Chapter Six 79
Angel from my Past: God's Protection in my Wilderness……………………………………..

EPILOGUE 83

AFTERWORD 89

ACKNOWLEDGEMENTS 93

ABOUT THE AUTHOR 95

INDEX 101

FOREWORD

Oftentimes in life, we wonder and question if God is truly present in our lives. His voice can be silent, and His actions subtle. We might even start thinking He's not there at all. This is one of the enemy's tricks in his arsenal. *Angels Among Us* illuminates God's handiwork in the life of one of His chosen children, Trudy Finney. As you read her personal accounts, watch as a single divine thread of yarn weaves in and out of her relationships, life choices, and thought processes. You will look up and realize a beautiful garment is being created at the hands of Father God, the master tailor.

Trudy's reflection provides transparent wisdom needed in this day and age. Her stories culminate in a powerful testimony of God's transformative power. You see her relationship evolve and grow with Christ through her missteps and triumphs. She shares moments of deep sorrow, horror, and great joy. She is authentic to who God called her to be and shares without an ounce of shame. You can feel the victory in her writing during the trial. It is like having a personal mother of the church take you by the hand and discipline you through their life's story. It then challenges you to consider your own divine thread in your own life.

I have the privilege of sharing personal space and time with Trudy. She is a woman of great faith, conviction, and passion. She truly loves the Lord. I do not say this lightly, but I have the opportunity to witness it on a day-to-day basis as we labor together in the ministry at *Legacy International Worship Center*. She is a pillar of strength and encouragement.

This book was birthed out of her desire to draw others to a relationship with Christ. This book is a weapon in our arsenal to combat the tricks of the enemy. I hear Trudy's voice cheering the reader on through the course of this book. What a gift she has given us. We can clearly see goodness and mercy following her all the days of her life. May we all see the *Angels Among Us*.

Co-Pastor First Lady, Amber Day

INTRODUCTION

In the quiet corners of a young girl's heart lies a storm that few can see. *Angels Among Us* invites you into this intimate space, where raw fears and crushing hopelessness threaten to drown out all hope.

You'll find yourself unable to look away as she navigates the treacherous waters of pain and loneliness. Each page will pull you deeper into her world—a world that might feel hauntingly familiar to your own hidden struggles.

Just when the darkness seems absolute, a whisper will break through. Divine love, persistent and unwavering, begins to illuminate the shadows. The promise that she is never truly alone transforms from mere words into a lifeline she clings to with both hands. This isn't just another tale of overcoming adversity; it's a visceral experience that will leave you breathless, tearful, and ultimately renewed. As you follow her transformation, you'll find yourself examining your own relationship with faith, hope, and the possibility of healing.

Clear your schedule before opening this book. You won't want to put it down until you've walked every step of this journey from desolation to deliverance.

Chapter One

"Even though I walk through the valley of the shadow of death, I will fear no evil, for you are with me; Your rod and Your staff, they comfort me." Psalm 23:4

My First Encounter with Angels: Crossing the Bridge

I grew up in South Jersey about thirty minutes from Philadelphia. I was 19 years old working in a small, local nursing home off Route 130 as a nurse's aide. It was my second job in a year, since graduating high school. It was a nice place with friendly people. The nursing director had a military background. She was a disciplined director, focused and fair. I admired that. I worked on the evening shift with mostly dementia patients. The work was hard but rewarding, but this is not the path I saw for myself. I never wanted to be a nurse. I wanted to be an artist.

In the 1980s, my career choice was to be a commercial artist. Today, it is called a graphic designer. That type of education was then, and is still now, expensive. I remember my mother and I traveling by bus to downtown Philadelphia. We had an appointment at the Art Institute with the financial aid department. We sat quietly, listening to the details of the money

Chapter One: My First Encounter with Angels

needed, loans that we could apply for or even receive some grants. I knew my mother was not going to apply for any loans. She did not like being in debt, and this would be a great debt for her. We thanked the financial advisor for her time and took all the paperwork to review and decide later. In truth though, that decision was already made in both of our minds; we just had not said it aloud yet. We waited for the bus to return home in silence. When we boarded the bus and sat down, my mother spoke with tears in her eyes. It was rare to see my mother tearing up.

"I'm sorry, but I can't help you," she said.

I was crushed. Not so much by the words she spoke—I understood the situation—but more so by her physical appearance, her body language, her facial expression. She looked absolutely defeated. I had never seen my mother like this. It was heartbreaking. I grabbed her hand and put my head on her shoulder.

"Don't worry, Mommy. I can get a job and save money for tuition. I can get a loan by myself without your help."

She really wasn't going to agree with what I was saying at all. She was afraid that if I didn't start school right away, I would get distracted.

My sisters and I visited the local employment agency. It was summer and we were starting our job hunting. My sisters are employed quickly, but I really did not have any skills. Finally, a lady found a position at a nursing facility in Cherry Hill. They were offering job training for a nurse's aide position. My heart sank. I could not imagine what the look on my face must have been, but I'm sure it didn't look like I was very grateful.

"A nurse? Can you please look again, I'll wait. There must be something else I can do."

The recruiter assigned to me was not very happy with me right about now.

"What's wrong with being a nurse? They are going to train you! I will look again but I don't think you're going to find anything better than this position."

Sure enough, there was nothing else. I accepted the position. I did not want to disappoint my mother after the promise I made, but I felt like I was being set up.

The challenge with taking this job was transportation. Although I had a driver's license, we had no car. No one wanted to take time out of their day to drive me to work, even if I offered to pay for gas. So, I had to take two buses and walk a few blocks to get there. This made me late every morning. It was a very bad start to what ended up being my life's career.

The nursing director who hired me was very gracious. She gave me time to find reliable

Chapter One: My First Encounter with Angels

transportation, In the meantime, I was trained in everything I needed to know for my job. I made a few friends and began to adjust to working with patients. The work was hard, and I learned quickly that not everyone worked as a team. Eventually, I made a friend who didn't mind giving me a ride to work in the mornings. I paid for gas, with a little extra for the inconvenience. Things were going well, and I started to feel more confident in what I was doing.

But one morning, I waited for my ride—and it never came. I had already missed the first bus, so that wasn't an option anymore. I was getting worried. I didn't know if there had been an accident or something else that had kept the girl from picking me up. I walked to a pay phone and called my job. I spoke with the nursing director and explained how worried I was. I told her I was sorry I wouldn't be able to arrive in time for my shift.

"Is the girl who works on my unit all right?" I asked. "Did she call to say what happened?"

It was silent for a moment. Then the director spoke.

"She arrived on time for her shift." She paused again before continuing. "I'm sorry, but I'm going to have to let you go. I just can't keep you any longer."

I could feel her genuine concern, and she truly seemed sorry. It took all my strength not to cry on the phone. I thanked her for giving me the opportunity and asked if I could use her as a reference for another job. She said she'd be more than happy to do me that favor, and then she wished me well.

I was devastated. My mother was right—I had gotten distracted. I hadn't saved any money. I wasn't living at home.

I started working closer to home at this facility that was on a local bus route. Dreams of art school faded quickly as more distractions took its place. I liked where I worked, and, in time, we received training to be certified as a nursing assistant by the state of New Jersey. Our military bred director sacrificed her own time at lunch and after work to help us all study for the exam. She furnished the study books, and we practiced the questions for a few months. When we were ready, we took a bus trip to Trenton to sit for the exam. I believe we all passed our exams. I was so happy; I was certified as a nursing assistant! I did not realize then just how important that little piece of paper would be for me later. All I knew was I finally stood still long enough to accomplish a goal. Outwardly, I was doing pretty good for myself. A young, black woman with a full-time job and a certification to her name. I was heading in the

Chapter One: My First Encounter with Angels

right direction, or was I? I was living with a man, and I was helping him. I was not in church anymore. Too ashamed to be near God. All my original plans fell apart, but God had His own plan.

Our meeting was by absolute chance. He was five years my senior and the size of a linebacker; 6ft. tall and 250 lbs. I learned he was a musician, loved boxing and was a sports car enthusiast. It wasn't that serious at first, I wasn't in love, but he was just always around. I could not understand why he was so interested. I'm sure he had other girlfriends. My eyes certainly roamed. But somehow time itself bound us. I left home at an early age and needed a place to stay. I went right to his door. This was absolutely a mistake! Things started out fine at first, but then it slowly changed into a controlling relationship.

My life with him was micromanaged with continuous threats. I believe once he realized he had power over me with fear, he no longer needed to put his hands on me. But the threat was always there. We ended up moving to Philadelphia, and I continued to work at the nursing home in New Jersey. I took the bus to work but the trick was getting back to that house at night. My shift ended at 11:30 p.m. The local public transportation did not run 24 hours like in Philadelphia, so my timing had to be correct. I had to catch a bus from my job to the Benjamin Franklin Bridge. There was a bus stop right before you cross the bridge. I waited there for the next bus to take me over into Philly. Then I walked to the subway station downtown to catch the light rail that dropped me off two blocks from where I lived.

This was my routine every night, and you best believe Mr. Man scrutinized every minute. Otherwise, I had to listen to the tirades, accusations, and threats. I would be up most of the night until he fell asleep drunk. I would start the process all over again the next day, hoping I did better.

The last bus arrived down the street from my job at 11:30 p.m., it left me off at the stop before the bridge. There was only about 10 minutes before the last bus to get over the bridge to Philly arrived. I was always relieved once I got downtown because I had more than one form of transportation to get back to the house. I liked the light rail; it dropped me off the closest to the house, and the driver was very nice. An older, fatherly-looking Black gentleman. He had a slim build, light brown skinned with salt and pepper hair. He was soft-spoken and always had a way to make me laugh. One time I saw him during the day driving the rail. I was with my significant other. When the driver noticed my companion and that I didn't speak just nodded, I

Chapter One: My First Encounter with Angels

believed my situation was put into perspective with him in an instant.

Coming home from work, I would always sit right behind his seat, and we talked the whole trip. Once I reached my stop, he always watched me walk two blocks until I turned the corner. We would wave to each other, and both disappear until the next night. By this time, it was almost 1 a.m. No one ever waited for me at that stop, only at the front door.

Work was routine. I had a few friends, but they did not know how I was living. On this particular night, I was gathering my belongings to get ready for the bus after my shift. One of my co-workers, a sweet enough looking elderly woman stopped me while I was preparing to leave. We didn't work in the same unit, but I was a little familiar with her. She said it was a shame I had to wait in the dark for the bus every night. She offered to give me a ride to my connecting bus to help me. She said it was on her way. I thought that was very kind of her, and I would save a little change. I accepted. She got herself ready, and we walked outside together.

There was a car blocking our path outside. I assumed we were about to walk to her car but instead she walked right up to the car in front of us and got in the from seat. I just stood there. I didn't understand what was going on. Then I heard her tell the woman in the driver seat that she promised me a ride. Apparently, this woman was her daughter who picked her up every night from work. My co-worker didn't drive. Her daughter was not pleased. She yelled at her mother then yelled at me to hurry up and get in! I must have been crazy. I got in the back seat. I figured with all the time it took to understand what was going on with these two, I probably already missed my first bus. I explained where I needed to go to catch my next bus. I was only familiar with the bus route which was pretty much a straight shot up Route 130 to the bridge. The closer you get to that stop there is a fork in the road. You can stay straight on Route 130 or go to the left on another road. She made the left. I told the lady that I wasn't familiar with this road, but she said it was all right to go this way. She drove quite a distance, and then she just stopped at a corner and said this was a bus stop. So, I got out.

    I couldn't believe it! I looked at that sweet old lady who offered me the ride. She just gave me a blank stare. She didn't even talk the entire ride. Now I'm out here on a street corner in Camden somewhere. It's about midnight now, and my next bus will be arriving. There were no houses around me, just large buildings and an empty lot in front of me. I can't wait here too long. I've already been standing here for 15 minutes, and I've seen no sign of life.

Chapter One: My First Encounter with Angels

Wait, there is a car coming up to the traffic light.

I got their attention and asked if they knew when the next bus was coming. They said no bus stops here and drove off.

Oh, my goodness! How did I get here?

I'm standing on a street corner in the dark with a white nursing dress on!

This is not happening to me right now!

How did I get here? That is really the question. My life wasn't like this a few years ago. I was home with my family. I went to church. I gave my heart to Jesus when I was 13 years old. I thought I had a plan, but for all sorts of painful and stupid reasons, I fell short. Got lost. Too many distractions. I couldn't hear God anymore; I was too far away. Now look at me, stuck on the corner with no ride trying to imagine what I will face whenever I do get back to the house.

Then suddenly, I realized I could see the bridge off to my right in the distance.

Maybe if I walk fast enough, I can figure out which way to go and make my bus.

The thought of walking was a little disturbing since it was so dark and eerily quiet. But before I could take the first step, I heard talking. In front of me there was an empty lot across the street. The streetlight was barely bright enough to illuminate the space, but I could make out three figures coming toward me, two men and a woman. I couldn't see their faces, but I could start to hear the conversation being about me. I froze in terror.

Were they going to rob me? I don't have anything to take but bus fare. As they got closer, I could see their faces, and I could tell whatever they were planning, it was not going to go in my favor. I looked to my right and thought maybe I could run but they were closing the distance and about to cross the street. Then suddenly, the smaller of the two male figures raised his hand to his side like he was pushing something back, and the others stopped walking. Next thing I know, he starts talking to me.

What kind of mess is this! I'm too scared to run now because he is getting too close.

"What?" He exclaimed. "That's my girl! I ain't seen you in a minute!"

I think I'm going to faint.

I looked at his companions, and they were still standing there. Now this guy has his arms out like he's going to touch me.

I stared right into his face, and he whispered, "Smile now."

So, I smiled, and he waved his friends off. "I'll catch up with y'all later."

He put his arm around me and said, "let's walk."

He asked, "What are you doing out here; you can get hurt."

At this point, I was shaking so hard he moved his arm from around me. He looked back to make sure his friends did not follow. I suddenly thought he must be the leader of this trio. I told him how I got there and that I needed to catch this bus or I'm in a lot of trouble. He said okay, and we started running together to the bus.

Let me stop for a minute because you really must picture this scene. Just a minute ago, I thought I was going to faint! I thought that I was about to be killed. Then this man starts acting like he knows me to get rid of the others. I should say a young black man about my age wearing all black and a hoodie. How can I best describe him? He was rough around the edges, he was hard looking, seriously thuggish. Not the type of person you want to run into on a dark quiet street. But here we are running together to catch my bus. Nobody but God, that is all I can say!

We ran because the bridge looked closer than it was. It had to be six to eight blocks. We finally got to the point where I had to just cross the road right in front of the bus stop. Not a typical road though, it was a multilane road where all the traffic is crossing the bridge in both directions. Fortunately for me, the traffic was light at that time of night. I thanked him for helping me; he had my life in his hands. I had nothing to offer him, but my bus fare, and I needed that. He smiled and said he didn't want anything, just hurry up and get across the road. So, I did with no problem. When I made it, I turned around, and *he was gone*. Tears came to my eyes. I thought, God please be with him. I often wonder if that soul still walks the earth with me. I pray God has touched his life.

Finally, I see the bus coming, but as it approaches it doesn't look familiar. Oh no! It's not my bus! The lighted sign on the front says, GARAGE. My heart sank. I flagged the bus down anyway. I asked the bus driver if he was going over the bridge. He said no, he was only going to the garage, his shift was over. I missed the bus I was waiting for. Then he drove off. I started to tremble with fear. I must walk over this bridge! First of all, I've never walked across a bridge like this one. The Benjamin Franklin Bridge spans almost two miles across, and its highest point is almost 400 feet high. It will take me at least 30 to 40 minutes to cross depending on how fast I walk. It's dark after midnight, and I must get downtown to Franklin Square to catch the light rail. I started walking fast. I was terrified! There was an inclination to this walk, and I just kept going higher and higher. Don't look down, just don't look

Chapter One: My First Encounter with Angels

down, I kept saying to myself. I didn't want to look back either, but then I wondered if someone else may also be walking over this bridge. I didn't want them to sneak up on me. I looked back, but no one was there.

Good. I looked ahead again and now there is a man approaching in the distance. Now I was sweating. My mind was racing with all the terrible things that could happen when he gets close enough to pass me. I was going crazy, and my heart was pounding.

I can't even swim! Not that it would matter from this height. Pull yourself together, Trudy. Be cool.

The strange man passed me walking fast with his head down, and I did the same. Although I did look back quickly just to make sure. I am really moving now. It seemed like I was walking for an eternity but now I can see 6th street.

I made it, I'm over bridge!

I checked my watch.

Oh no, I have minutes to spare. I'm not going to make it.

I started running to the station.

I'm not going to make it, I'm late.

I had a flight of steps to run down and round a corner. I felt my eyes filling with tears.

I'm not going to make it.

When I got to my spot, the trolly was there with the doors open. Just sitting there. I couldn't believe it. I cautiously walked up to the open door, and there was my regular driver sitting there smiling at me.

He said, "I figured you were late, and I didn't want to leave you."

I stood there drenched in sweat, not believing my eyes or my ears.

I just started laughing and told him, "Yeah, I missed my bus."

What an Angel!

He let me off at my regular stop at my usual time. Don't ask me how that happened, but you know who had me in His hands.

Chapter Two

"He lifted me out of the pit of despair, out of the mud and the mire. He set my feet on solid ground and steadied me as I walked along." Psalm 40:2

God's Deliverance from Death: His Voice

The rest of the year slowly dragged on with this man, and I was seriously losing my identity. I found myself losing sight of God. With every unwise decision, with every stumble, with every fall, the distance between God and I was great. I could not see Him. I could not hear Him.

To survive my torment, I had taken on the personality of my oppressor. Since every word I spoke and every action I took was closely scrutinized and summed up as stupidity, laced with threats, I just laid who I was to rest. To escape the fear of bodily harm and mental anguish, I became my oppressor. I agreed with everything he said as truth. If he lied, then I lied to protect him. If he hurt others, I was right by his side. In doing so I had a moment of calm with him. You see, he was pleased with my new behavior. There was no need for him to yell at me or put his hands on me. I am sure in his mind, he felt he was quite successful in breaking me. Here is the problem though, it was a very painful process for me. This was not my nature. It was all an act to protect myself, but I was losing my mind. My conflict now was with myself. Not only that but I was seeing a more violent side to this man. I was being ignored. My only purpose was to provide. He was unemployed and unemployable.

His nature was one of cruelty towards others. Starting fights without a thought, he was rogue. It is only by the grace of God he was never able get his hands on a gun, at least not while I was with him. In the meantime, I was spiraling downward into dark places in my mind. I wanted out!

Go home, one might say. No, there was a reason I left, so no going back. Go somewhere else. Where?

I am now trapped in my own mind. I built this prison of confusion around myself. The bars are nothing more than the lies of the enemy that I began to believe.

One night, I was watching the news. A woman committed suicide, and her husband went to prison for her murder. It didn't make sense to me. I don't remember all the details, but she wrote in her diary about all his abuse. It must have been convincing enough for a judge to convict this man of murder for leading his wife to take her own life to escape him.

Believe me, at this moment, my thoughts were not on God. The door just flew open for the enemy to take control and twist my thoughts in relation to my own situation.

I was angry! This poor woman had to die for someone to take notice to her plight, but at least, I thought, he was being punished. I was angry because with all my "bad girl" role play, I was being used and insulted more than ever. This man had no job. He had no car. I had the car, but I could never drive it. He kept the keys. He drove me to work, dropped me off and picked me up. He was with me everywhere I went, especially to the bank when I cashed my check and paid the bills.

This needs to end! I am going to make him pay!

Did I suddenly have a bag of courage fall on my head? No. Here is the lie I believed:

I am worthless. I cannot go back to my life. I ruined my life with disobedience, fear, shame. I stopped caring about myself a long time ago. I will not burden my mother any longer with this child she probably didn't want or planned for, a mistake. It is ok, it's time for me to pay for all my sins. I am not even good enough for God now but at least this man who I let torment me will suffer. I never believed I would live past 20 years of age anyway.

Chapter Two: God's Deliverance from Death

I will not get into the details of my planning, means and opportunity. The devil is a liar, so let us get to God's truth!

Everything was set in motion. It was my night off. I was working a new job in Philadelphia, so there were no more bus trips. Now I am escorted to and from work on the evening shift. But tonight, I was home alone, and Mr. Man was out doing whatever he does with my car. Anyway, I knew I had some time to get this over with. I bought a new dress that I have never worn before. It was beautiful! Cream colored with lots of lace. I love lace. I took a bath and let out my hair. I wanted to look nice for my sleep. I needed to write a note. I got some paper and a pen and went blank on what to say. I'll write it later, or not. I laid the paper and pen down on the dresser. All the lights in the apartment were off. No TV, no music, nothing. I realized, my mind was still. I had no fear but just the thought of sleeping, finally getting some rest. Remember, the devil is a liar. My dress was laid out on the bed, I imagined myself in it, looking very pretty. What should I do first, I thought, drink this stuff then get dressed or the other way around. I decided to drink.

Then something happened. Do you remember when you were a kid playing outside with your friends and you knew before the streetlight came on, you had better be in the house, and if not, that was your butt? The last thing you wanted to hear while you were with your friends was your name being called. So embarrassing. But that was the running joke for us kids back then. We would all try to imitate our parents calling us. The way they would enunciate our names in the heat of anger.

Some kids said they knew they were in trouble if their parents called them by their first, middle, and last name. Others said their parents would drag their name out, or maybe it was just a certain tone of their voice that they didn't normally use. I tried to imitate the way my mom called me out, but it was too hard. She had a slight Caribbean accent that I could never imitate. But make no mistake, her tone, accent and all, let you know she was not playing with you, and she was not going to call you a second time!

Before I could open my mouth, to take my drink, I heard my name being called out! Very loud and very clear!

"Trudy!"

What! Mommy's here!

The fear in me felt like I just got a barrel of ice water poured over me. And at the same time, I was almost relieved.

I ran into the living room, turned on the light, and yelled out, "Mommy!"

But when the light came on, she wasn't there.

Where is she? She just called me, in that tone like I am in trouble. Like, what are you doing? What am I doing? My mother is in another state, she does not know this address.

Somebody just snapped their fingers and woke me from a trance. That's what it felt like.

No, no, no I'm not crazy—my mother just called me!

Then I realized what just happened. I ran back to the bedroom, turned on the light, and went down on my knees by my bed.

"Lord forgive me, Lord I'm sorry! I will never think of doing such a thing again! Lord!"

I cried so hard!

What was I thinking? I just heard God call my name—using my mother's voice! Ha! God can do whatever He wants!

I was happy—crazy happy! I ran back into the living room. The light was still on and nobody was there! I felt drunk. But then I heard something else—not audible but in my mind: *Hurry up! Clean up! He will be home soon.*

So, I did. I hung up that dress. I cleaned up the mess I made when I dropped what was in my hands when I heard my name. I put on my pajamas.

Now write this down.

Write what? I grabbed the pen and paper I left on the dresser, jumped on the bed, and started writing instructions, I numbered each one: how to pack, what to pack, where to hide it until I left, how much money I needed. Not much—it would give me away. I wrote every detail down, but a few things were missing: Where was I going? How was I going to get there? And when can I leave?

I want to leave right now!

No. He is coming.

I turned on the TV, jumped on the couch and tried very hard to contain my excitement. I am out of here, all right. I just don't know when I'm leaving.

I know what you are thinking, I just said I heard the voice of God. Yes, I did, loudly and with authority, hear my name! I was terrified, shaking, crying on my knees, praying for forgiveness. It was amazing! That was a one-time deal for me. It never happened again. I did not know it then, but I realize it now. The Holy Spirit took over after that, giving me instructions. That voice in my head telling me what to do. Now He has my attention.

The days turned into weeks, and I continued to check and follow my list. It all starts with my daily routine. I work the evening shift, so I get ready for work and throw things I need for work in my duffle bag. I carry a duffle bag around because I don't want to be robbed wearing a purse. Especially if I have to walk to work, which happens often. I usually pack my lunch, a sweater and my mail as we leave. I get dropped off at work in the front of the building and get picked up at the same spot. On pay days, I'm escorted to pick up my check at work. This is very embarrassing, since my co-workers can't believe the "beast" I'm walking with through the building. "Is that her man?" I'm sure that's what they're thinking. Next, it's off to the bank to cash the check and buy money orders for the bills. All under the watchful eye of my escort.

So how do I accomplish what's on this list? Easy, very carefully. First, I have to pack. I had two duffle bags, so I started folding one of them up and putting them into the other. I also wrapped a few items of underwear into my sweater. I would hide the important documents I need to take in a magazine. Birth certificate, important phone numbers and addresses, all the documents that had to do with my car. I took as much paperwork as possible so I could start over. I didn't want to forget anything. Lastly, I would always take the mail with me, which had to be part of the routine, I wanted to have all of my bills. I did this every day, a little at a time so he wouldn't notice. What's funny is, as much as he tried to watch me, he never checked my bag, amazing. Now when I arrived at work, I put the bag in my locker with all of the items and brought the other bag home with the usual stuff in it. Every day I would just take items from one bag and pack them into the other bag in my locker. It took forever but I did it. Almost everything was checked off my list, but I still didn't know where I was going or when.

One evening watching the news, I saw a story about a trolly either derailing or in some type of accident in a Pittsburgh neighborhood. I don't know why this caught my attention, but it did.

Pittsburgh. Where the heck is Pittsburgh?!

Sounds funny now, but back then, I really didn't know anything about Pittsburgh. I wasn't a big sports fan, and I didn't know anyone who said they were from that area. So, for the next couple of days, all I could think about was Pittsburgh. When I got to work, I found a map and looked it up. It was all the way on the other side of Pennsylvania. That should be far enough, I thought. I will still be in Pennsylvania, and I wouldn't have to get a new driver's license.

Why Pittsburgh? I thought. *I could go anywhere in the country. I had family and friends in other states. But the problem is Mr. Man knows all these folks and where they live. Oh, he will harass them after I'm gone. I'm sure of it!. He doesn't know anyone in Pittsburgh. I've never heard his family talk about Pittsburgh. It's settled, I'm going to Pittsburgh, and the cheapest way to go is by Greyhound. Now I can check that off my list. Now, when can I leave?*

This game I play with this man is getting exhausting. I feel like I'm in a movie where the wives are robots or something, no soul, no personality. Except I'm the human wife who's just pretending to get by and survive.

The Thanksgiving holiday was fast approaching, and I was trying not to get depressed.

I'm still here with no clear escape route yet.

Suddenly Mr. Man gets the idea that he wants company over for Thanksgiving, and I am to cook and entertain.

This can't be happening!

Is he so comfortable with our situation that he's pretending to be some type of family man? I really can't deal with this. I can't believe this is going to happen, and I must act happily about it.

"Oh, that's a wonderful idea."

Help me, Lord!

My only escape these days is going to work. I have two good friends that mean the world to me. They're both older than me, probably old enough to be my parents, but they were so cool! The three of us worked in the same unit, and we were always together. They had strong personalities and beautiful souls. At work, I put on my tough skin too because some of my co-workers were rough, but the three of us together were a force to be reckoned with. I couldn't have survived in that place without them.

Roxy was a fun-loving free spirit. She couldn't be broken. She always made me laugh, but believe me, she was no joke. I wouldn't want to make her mad. Murphy was more serious. She liked being called by her last name. She was more laid back about things. The voice of reason. They were my work mothers. They always had my back, and I loved them both. But, as much as I trusted them, I didn't tell them what I was going through. I think they started to suspect something was up whenever I would go off by myself to figure out my list, getting the plan in order. I couldn't tell them what I was doing. It was better that way. I knew the wrath that would follow, and it would be better for them not to know than they try to lie and cover for me. So, I told no one. Not even my mother.

Thanksgiving was in a couple of weeks, and I was stressed. Roxy and Murphy were talking about their holiday plans. I figured I should get some quick recipes from them to try since I needed to cook dinner. While we're going over recipes, one of our co-workers told us there was an emergency union meeting tomorrow about an upcoming strike.

What?! This is crazy. Now what do I do? I can't lose my job—not yet anyway.

At the meeting, it was explained that we are striking for better wages, healthcare and things like that.

I can't believe what I'm hearing.

I was getting very anxious about it all, but I was trying to play it cool. Roxy and Murphy were looking forward to it. It didn't seem to bother them at all. We were going to strike after Thanksgiving. We would have one more meeting before the evening shift on that Friday and strike on Saturday. Murphy tried to reassure me that everything would be alright. The residents will go to their families or other facilities for care before the strike starts.

"Our work assignments will get light with so many patients being sent out. Believe me it will be a short strike, and we'll get what we want. Most of these families either don't want to or can't take care of their loved ones."

I tried to calm down, but it was hard. Then that voice came back: *You're leaving after Thanksgiving.*

Hmmm. I'm leaving after Thanksgiving. Well, that just happens to be a pay week. I will get paid early because of the holiday. So, pay day is Wednesday. I will have time to figure out my travel money and groceries for the holiday dinner. The meeting is before our shift on Friday. Mr. Man knows about the strike, but he doesn't know about the early meeting. Now I know when I'm leaving, great! Now, how do I do this?

One of the items on my list was writing a letter to my supervisor. So, on my dinner break at work I wrote a short letter, I said something like, "I apologize for leaving without notice, but I am involved in some circumstances that are beyond my control. I appreciate the time that I have worked here, and I hope that you can give a good reference for me in the future."

I put it in an envelope, addressed it to my supervisor and sealed it. I later put the letter in my locker next to my packed bag. Everything was checked off my list. I was ready.

Wednesday before Thanksgiving was payday. We played out our usual routine. We picked up the check. We went to the bank to cash the check and pay for the money orders for the utilities. But this part was not routine. I needed money to travel and survive. I made a list of the money order amounts on a piece of paper to give to the teller as I always do. It's usually the same teller. A young lady who quickly noticed how Mr. Man hovers over me like Lurch, watching my every move. She always smiles at me but pretty much ignores him. On this day, all the money order amounts were the same: $20.00. She looked up at me but before she opened her mouth, I slightly shook my head and winked at her. She looked at me nervously, but then she noticed that he wasn't standing next to me. The teller tilted her head to the side, and then I looked in that direction.

Well, what do you know? Mr. Man is so comfortable with this routine he has found interest in a pretty little thing on the other side of the room. They're just chatting it up. I love it!

I smiled back at the teller and hurried to write out my money orders. Everybody I owed got $20.00. I kept the rest. The teller gave me the balance back in cash in a separate envelope. That went in my pocket. By the time he remembered me, I was ready to go. I acted like I had no idea he was talking to anyone. We left and went grocery shopping.

On Thanksgiving morning, I got up early and started cooking. We had four guests come over. Everything went fine, no arguments, no fine tuning of every move I made in the kitchen, just peace. I think he was showing off. I was genuinely happy, because I knew something he didn't. Oh, Glory to God!

Friday after Thanksgiving, I started getting myself ready for work. The only thing he noticed that was out of the ordinary was how much food I was packing for my dinner. As if he wouldn't have enough for himself. We went downstairs to the mailbox, got the mail, and then we left at my usual time.

He dropped me off at work at the front door. There wasn't anyone around.

I said my usual, "I'll see you tonight."

I watched him drive away in my car.

Oh well. Now this is the tricky part. I know everyone is at the meeting, and I should be able to get down to the locker room unnoticed.

I took the back stairs trying to avoid the meeting area. No one was in the locker room. I got my bag and the letter for my supervisor.

I have to drop this letter off, and her office is on the other side of the building. There is a chance I may run into someone, but here it goes.

The hallway to the administrative offices was clear—or so I thought.

"Trudy, where are you going? The meeting is the other way."

It was one of the clerks in the office.

"Oh yes, I know, but I have a message to give the supervisor before I go to the meeting."

"Well, she's not in her office right now," the clerk said. "I'll give it to her."

Chapter Two: God's Deliverance from Death

"No, "I averted. "I'll just stick it under her door, but thanks."

"Okay, well hurry up. You're already late."

I took my time before leaving the office to make sure the clerk was gone. When it was clear, I ran back down the steps. My plan was to get out the side door, across the street and through a residential neighborhood that leads back to City Line Avenue and the bus stop. It was all smooth as butter until I ran into Roxy crossing the street.

"Trudy, where are you going?"

I can't believe it! I have to think of a quick story.

"Hi," I exclaim. "Oh, I'll be back. I forgot something at home. I'll just be a little late. Don't worry!"

I almost said "good-bye," but I caught myself. I could tell by the look on her face that she didn't believe or understand anything I just said to her. She almost looked at me like she knew she would never see me again. I hurried past her to get down the street, but I felt the tears filling me up. I was so scared.

What if he was still driving around? What if he doubled back for some reason? I couldn't be seen again.

I approached the bus stop. There were a few people standing there but I didn't stand next to them. I sort of stood back near a tree, so I wasn't seen on the road. When the bus came, I jumped on with everyone else. I kept my head down and didn't look at anyone. You never know who you may run into. He had a lot of friends and family in the area.

I got off the bus downtown near the Greyhound station. On the same block was the branch of my local bank. I needed to close out my account this time. Not that I had much in my account, but it was mine, and I needed it.

At what must be four or five in the evening, I walked into the bus station, and it's packed. When I saw all the people, I panicked.

I hoped no one recognizes me.

I purchased my one-way ticket and sat down away from the crowd. I had to wait an hour. I thought I would lose my mind. Finally, the bus arrived.

Most of these folks are getting on the same bus! I better get a seat; I'm not waiting on another bus.

Chapter Three

"Behold, I am going to send an angel before you to guard you along the way and to bring you into the place which I prepared." Exodus 23:20

Road Trip Angel

The line formed quickly, and I was near the end. Once on the bus, I didn't see any open seats right away. I saw some people sitting on the aisle with an empty window seat.

Oh my, here goes.

The winning smile broke out as I looked at each person for a seat. Most were less than polite; some rolled their eyes. But this guy to my right was sitting in the window seat. When he noticed me, he jumped up with a bigger smile than I was wearing. He looked a little rough but clean.

A late 20's, early 30's looking white guy. He had a smile that looked like a few teeth got knocked out. He moved all his belongings so I could have the window seat. The people behind me weren't that happy about the hold up. This man looked at the crowd, said a few choice words and then waited for one of them to answer him. They did not. He turned back on his charm towards me, and I rushed into my seat. I really wanted to sit on the aisle, but I wasn't going to complain after that display of hostility. We had a moment of silence and smiles, and then he asked me where I was going. We exchanged our names, and then the conversation began. Silence was broken for the next six hours or so. I've never been on such a long bus ride. We talked about everything he could think of. He did most of the talking. Where was I from? Where am I going?

"Oh, I'm from Pittsburgh. I can tell you all about Pittsburgh."

And he did exactly that! Finally, I got a word in and asked my own questions.

"Where are you coming from?"

He was coming from Miami. He was just let out of prison. In the 1980's, Florida had a problem with overcrowded prisons. The governor declared a state of emergency and began to release some non-dangerous prisoners. So, he's going back home. *Oh my, I'm trying not to let my imagination run away.*

"So," I asked, "why were you in prison?"

"Drug possession."

I thought to myself. *That sounds pretty vague.* But I didn't want to know any more than that right then.

No doubt there is more to that story.

For the next few hours, I was treated as one who needed protection. People probably thought we were a couple.

I just tried to play it cool. He had to call his parole officer at every stop, and he had a certain amount of time to make that call. He told me he could stay with his family tonight but had to go to the halfway house in the morning to live. We were getting closer to the city, and I was getting excited. I booked a room at a hotel that I thought was in the downtown area. I had about $500 on me so I needed to be smart about my spending. I didn't even eat the whole trip, just snacks. My new friend asked where I was going to stay tonight. I thought I was going to faint. My mouth got so dry I couldn't get my words out right away.

"Oh, a hotel downtown."

"What's the address?"

"I can tell you where it is."

I was nervous but I gave him the address I copied out of the phonebook.

"Downtown! This isn't downtown. This is like at least 15 to 20 minutes from downtown."

My heart sank, now what was I going to do? Well, my new friend was gracious enough to offer me a ride. He said his mother was going to be at the bus station to pick him up.

Chapter Three: Road Trip Angel

"The hotel will be on the way."

I tried very hard not to shake in front of him. I don't know this man. He just got out of prison; now I'm going to get in the car with him and his family!

"Thanks, but I'll get a cab."

"They're too expensive. Anyway, you don't have to pay my mom. She wouldn't think of it."

We finally got to the station, got our bags, and were about to walk out. Right before we got to the door, my friend warned me that there would be a lot of guys outside who drive Jitney's, and they just come at you to get you to ride with them. I never heard of a Jitney, but I just acted like I knew what he was talking about. Once we walked out of the door, I realized what he meant. They were right in my face, but my friend shooed them away. Suddenly he spoke up.

"There she is: my mom!"

She pulled right up to the curb, jumped out of the car and ran to hug him.

She was a petite little elderly woman with grey hair. She looked over at me with the biggest smile.

"Who is this?"

He explained who I was and that I needed a ride. "Oh, sure, honey! That's no problem; it's on the way!"

I kind of felt at ease after meeting his mother, then I realized there was one more person in the car.

His brother. He didn't get out of the car to greet him. My friend and I got into the back seat. He gave me a formal introduction of his mom and brother, and then we left. His brother didn't say anything to me, but he did turn himself around in his seat to stare at me. I really didn't like it, but I tried to play it off. My friend and his mother talked so much I don't think they noticed this man's posture toward me. I was so irritated I decided to stare back, with an attitude! Finally, the tension was noticed by both my friend and his mom, and after being cursed at by both, his brother finally turned around.

"Don't mind him."

Easy for him to say, I thought.

It seemed like the longest 20-minute ride in the world. It's almost 1 a.m., and I can't believe I'm in Pittsburgh or at least the surrounding area! The car pulled up to the hotel. I was so excited, I just wanted to jump out of the car and run!

But I didn't. I thanked them for the ride and was grateful to my travel companion. Who knows how many jerks he kept away from me during this journey? After the goodbyes were said, there seemed to be a moment of awkward silence where everybody was smiling at me. Suddenly, my friend says, "Mom give me a piece of paper and pen, hurry up!"

The next thing I know, I now have his mother's phone number, and the number at the halfway house.

"Well ok, yeah, thanks for everything!" He wouldn't stop smiling at me, so I gave him a hug and a quick kiss on the cheek and jumped out of the car.

I must be crazy. Yes I've lost my mind!

I waved goodbye and hurried to the hotel. I checked in, got my keys and locked the door behind me. Suddenly I felt weak. All the adrenaline just drained from my body. I fell on the bed feeling numb.

Oh, my goodness! Now what?

I took a bath, changed into my pajamas, spread out my Thanksgiving dinner, and ate it all!

Chapter Four

"I remain confident of this: I will see the goodness of the Lord in the land of the living." Psalm 27:13

Hotel Angels

Evergreen

The next morning, I got up early. I had to figure out where I was and get back to town. The hotel clerk said I was in the South Hills of Pittsburgh on Banksville Road. That didn't mean a whole lot to me at the time, but I grabbed my favorite go-to for information: the phone book. Don't laugh. That's all I had. Also, something called a "green sheet" that the clerk gave me.

I told him I needed to find a place to stay because I didn't budget to stay another night in this hotel. I scanned through so many places, but nothing was right. Too expensive, too far away. Then I spotted this place that was a hotel that I could pay for monthly rent for a room. I asked the hotel clerk if he ever heard of this place.

"Yes," he said. "It's a nice area on the bus route."

"Is it close to downtown?"

"All the buses go downtown."

Chapter Four: Hotel Angels

I called this place up, and they had rooms available. I was so happy!

I told them I was on my way. I checked out of the hotel and called for a cab to pick me up. The cab arrived, and he was very nice to me. He said I would love Pittsburgh; the people are friendly.

That's encouraging, I thought. *I'm a 20-year-old black woman, and so far, I haven't seen many people who look like me. No problem. I haven't really seen anything yet.*

The city was beautiful with rivers and bridges. It was a gorgeous, fall day! I just felt this new life in me.

I can't remember the last time I felt like this!

The ride seemed shorter than it was the night before. We seemed to pass by downtown, so I asked what part of the city we are going to.

"North Hills," he said. "But you're on the bus route, so all the buses go downtown."

We pulled up to this structure that looked like it had been standing since the beginning of time. It was old and big and a little scary looking. I paid the driver and got out of the cab.

Apparently, this place is a bar, restaurant, and hotel. It seems to sit in the middle of nowhere.

I walked through the door to the restaurant.

I was surprised to see such a beautiful interior. As soon as I entered, I faced a long bar with lovely woodwork. At the end of the bar, I could see a door that opens to a large kitchen. The rest of the space was a large dining room with small tables. Toward the back of the dining room to the right was a spiral staircase. It seemed like a strange place for a staircase. I wondered where it led.

I sat down at the bar and two young women came out of the kitchen. They looked like my age, maybe a little older. I told them I was answering the ad for a room to rent, but I wanted to know the price for a month's stay.

One of the girls said she would bring the owner out to talk to me. They seemed very friendly, all smiles in fact. I could see the curiosity in their eyes. They were probably wondering where in the world I came from. The owner arrived. He was tall man with dark hair and not much expression on his face. Very serious and almost weighed down looking. His voice was almost monotone. He gave me the rate for a month's rent at $150. I agreed.

There goes a big chunk of my money. I had to be very careful how I spent what was left.

I asked him where the spiral staircase goes. He stared at me for a second and then told me no one uses those stairs. They lead to the second floor where residents live. To access the main house, you must go back outside and let yourself in the front door. He was ready to lead me to my room, but before we walked out, one of the girls said to come back down after I was settled. We walked outside and to the left to the main house.

The bar appeared to be an addition to the older structure. I stood in front of what seemed to be a million wide stair steps to climb. For a moment, I felt like I was in a seen from the movie, *Psycho*. This house was dark and very creepy. But again, the woodwork caught my eye. This place must have been grand back in its day. We went up to the second floor and the windows brought in more light, so it didn't look so bad up there. We walked down the hall to the left, and he opened the room door and gave me the keys. He pointed to the community bathroom a little further down the hall to the right. He told me if I needed anything or had any trouble to let him know.

Have any trouble? I thought.

I landed in a semi-rural area, which is predominately white in population, and the last black person I remember seeing was at the bus station last night.

Oh, I'll let him know, alright!

The room was big with a twin bed, a nightstand with a radio and a chair. It was very bright due to the big window, and there was a small closet. It's early in the day and very quiet, but I know other people must live here, I just didn't know how many and how close they were to my room. I turned on the radio, trying to find something familiar sounding, but there were a lot of country music stations. I thought there must be a black radio station somewhere but before I could find it, I heard a broadcast of a parade going on downtown. It was called *Holiday Parade*. I listened to that and laid down on the bed. I almost forgot it was the holiday.

Suddenly, the heaviness of everything I just went through covered me! I started to cry.

"Oh, God! Are you still here with me? I can't hear you. I must snap out of it! I have thirty days to come up with a plan. I can't stay here."

I went back downstairs to talk to the girls I just met. I need to get some information out of them so I can navigate my new city. Well, it's more like a big town. I went back to the bar and struck up a conversation with my new friends. They really were friendly. They told me everything I needed to know about Pittsburgh. I had to start taking notes. Apparently, the place I was staying at was once a historical landmark, built in the 1800's. Over the years and multiple owners, it seemed to lose its charm. This place has a history, but I seemed to have arrived before any of its real problems started.

Chapter Four: Hotel Angels

I was told about the different neighborhoods, the sports, the night life, the food, everything. I wanted to know about public transportation. They gave me information about the buses and the light rail downtown, but that only went to the South Hills I found out later. I asked about the trollies because I saw them on TV. They had already gotten rid of the trolley system, but there were a few inclines. They explained to me how to get downtown by bus and gave me a few bus schedules. I would later learn how to master these schedules and go wherever I wanted. The nearest grocery store was right down the road. I wondered if I could walk the distance because I couldn't see it from outside of the bar. I remember mentioning something about picking up a Sunday paper to look for jobs and my next place to live. I was starting to feel a little better, even excited.

One of the girls asked me what room I was in, and I told her. Then I said my goodbyes and headed back to my room. As I approached the door, I saw a white man going into the bathroom, he just stared at me as he walked through doorway. I quickly got into my room and locked the door. I put the chair against the door under the doorknob. I always wondered if that really worked, but I guess it would buy me a little time.

It always seemed to work on TV. A few minutes later, there was a knock at the door. It was the owner.

"I got a better room for you with your own bathroom. Same price."

"Thank you," I said.

I gathered the little I had and followed him up to the next floor. He took me to the very end of a hallway by a big window. He gave me new keys and let me in. Again, he said if I needed him to let him know. But this time he said,

"Or you can tell my mother. She lives right next door to you across the hall."

"Thank you so much!"

He didn't have much else to say, he just walked away. This was a nice room. Old, of course, like everything else but clean. And, I had my own bathroom with a shower. It's just the little things sometimes that make all the difference.

I didn't come out of my room for the rest of the day. When night fell, I was so tired, I went to bed with my stomach growling and my heart still heavy. I figured tomorrow I would start the countdown on how I would get out of there with a job and a new place to live. I prayed and fell asleep.

Chapter Four: Hotel Angels

Today is Sunday, and I woke up feeling excited to explore my new home. I wanted to walk around and find the grocery store. I needed the Sunday paper and a few cheap food items. Once I had that, I could start my research on Pittsburgh.

On my way out of the building, I exited out of a side door and ran into a man entering. We exchanged good mornings, and then I asked if he knew how far the grocery store was from there. He gave me directions, and I was on my way. It was a nice little walk from the hotel down the road that I now know to be Babcock Blvd. As soon as I walked in, I found the green sheet. I still got a Sunday paper, as well as a notebook and pen, a couple bottles of water, two small hoagies, some crackers, and a small jar of peanut butter. I didn't want to carry or spend too much.

I walked back to the hotel and back up to my room. I just put everything down and there was a knock on the door.

I didn't see anyone around when I walked in, so who could that be?

I asked who it was, and I heard a woman's voice. I opened the door, and it was the owner's mother from across the hall. She introduced herself and said if I ever have anything to put in her fridge to keep cold, just knock on her door. Then whenever I was ready for it, I could come and get it.

"Thank you so much," I beamed.

I realized her room door was open as we were talking, but her room was a nice apartment. She must have seen me going to the store. I gave her my hoagies, and we parted ways. I was so happy she was right across the hall.

I started to settle in, spreading out my research items on the bed. Notebook, pen, newspapers and a bus schedule. I was ready to start when there was another knock on my door.

Oh, that sweet little lady must want to tell me something.

I jumped up and opened the door, it wasn't her.

It was the guy that gave me directions earlier this morning. He stood there with a stupid grin on his face, and a bottle of Heineken in each hand. I was confused at this site but before I could say anything, he shoved a bottle of beer in my hand.

"Welcome to the neighborhood," he grinned.

"Wow, thanks, thank you very much!"

That's all I could think of saying with a half-smile. Then I proceeded to close my door. I was shocked when he stuck his foot in the door.

"Aren't you going to let me in? I just gave you a beer!"

Chapter Four: Hotel Angels

The fire rose up in me, my attitude got twisted really fast. My smile faded, and I repositioned the bottle in my left hand. I swung open the door and literally stepped to the man and told him to back up! He had a look of shock on his face, but he backed up, and I slammed the door. I grabbed the chair and stuck it under the doorknob.

Really! I'm sweating now! I'm mad! Does he think I'm a prostitute? The thought made me angry! I started pacing the room, half thinking this man may come right back. I waited for a while trying to see what was in the room I could use for a weapon. The lamp? The bottle of beer? There wasn't much else.

He didn't come back, and I thought, *You know what? I'm just going to tell the owner. I might need to leave here a lot sooner than I thought. Wait, I can't do that, I've barely been here two days.*

I left the room in search of the owner and found him in the dining room downstairs.

I told him what happened and described the man to him. It turns out this guy helps him around the place sometimes, but he doesn't live there.

"Don't worry," he said." I'll talk to him, but don't worry, you won't see him again."

He looked at me with sort of flat affect mixed with an attitude.

I could never read him, so I said, "Ok, thanks."

True to his words, I never saw that guy again for the remainder of my stay. I went back to my room and knocked on my neighbor's door to retrieve one of my hoagies. She greeted me with a smile and gave me my food. I always wondered if she heard all the commotion.

I finally finished looking at the paper, searching for jobs, apartments or rooms for rent. I looked for anything with a map and whatever was going on in the city. I made a list of things to do and look for downtown. I was excited to go explore my new home. *Now I'm hungry.* I started to eat my hoagie dinner. I looked over at the beer and thought this was a cause for celebration. I survived two days.

9th Street

I slept well last night. No crying, no worry, just knocked out cold. It must have been the beer, but I'm ready for the day. The bus stop was right in front of the hotel. I was so excited to explore I think I talked the poor bus driver to death. As we were driving, I saw some sort of construction going on down below our road. It was just mountains of dirt and heavy equipment. I asked the bus driver what was going on down there. He said there is a new highway being built. I have never seen anything like it. It's now part of I-279.

Once I arrived downtown, it was like a whole new world to discover. It wasn't like New York, busy and crowded. It wasn't like Philly either. It was just a big town, and I loved it! It was so easy to walk around. It didn't take me long to find what I needed.

First stop was a pawn shop. I needed money, so I sold my stupid engagement ring, from Mr. Man, and my high school class ring. I didn't get much for the class ring. *Now I regret purchasing a cute little white gold ring. I would have gotten a lot more if I bought the big bulky yellow gold ring. Oh well.* This was enough to get a monthly bus pass, which was about $50.00. *I'll get a nice lunch and hold on to the rest.*

I walked up to a small restaurant with a sign that advertised Gyros. I didn't know what a gyro was, but I was about to find out because the aroma coming out of this place was amazing! After lunch, I walked around to different small businesses to fill out applications for employment. The only skill I had was as a nursing assistant. I knew I could get a job with this skill, but I needed money now. I didn't have a car to get around, and I need a little more time to study these bus schedules to get from point A to point B.

I came downtown everyday filling out applications. I was able to use the hotel's phone number for a point of contact. The bar maids were so nice to me, they promised to take any messages that came through. But I didn't hear anything back from any of them. I was starting to get discouraged, but I kept my routine going. It was a cold December day when I started noticing how people were looking at me as I walked. Even when I asked for applications the store clerks looked at me funny. They either didn't want to touch me when handing me the applications or they just said we're not hiring.

As I walked around, I started wondering what I looked like to them all. I was clean, my hair was combed, my clothes were a little baggy, but I thought I looked presentable. That was until an elderly woman came up to me and asked me if I was warm enough because of the jacket I was wearing looked thin. I was so embarrassed; I almost started to cry. I assured her that I was just fine and that I grabbed the wrong coat on my way out the door. When she walked away, I just wanted to run. I was freezing, with no hat, no gloves, and no scarf. I couldn't spend my money on those things. I had to hold on to what I had until I got a job.

Every day I became more depressed and lonelier. I couldn't sleep at night because my mind would just race from one thing to the other. After coming back to the hotel from downtown every evening, I was so bored. I sat in my room going crazy because I knew how endless the night would feel. One morning before heading out for the bus, the barmaid said she never sees me anymore. She suggested that I come down and talk sometimes before it gets too busy in the bar.

Yeah sure, I can do that. I never thought to do that before, why not.

That evening, I went down to the bar. The TV was on, and I watched the news. There were baskets of chips and pretzels set out for free. It looks like dinner to me. One of the girls asked if I wanted something to drink.

"Water, is that free?"

She laughed! "Yes, water is free, but I was talking about something stronger."

"Oh, I can't afford anything like that, but thanks."

I started to feel a little more human socializing with the girls working at the bar and watching TV.

I was having fun—then Happy Hour kicked in to full swing. This is when things started to get real, in this place. The girls got busy all right. I always sat at the end of the bar near the door so I would be out of the way, hoping not to be noticed. That was a joke, I was the only black person in there. I came down to the bar every evening to watch the news, drink water and eat chips and pretzels but I didn't leave until 1 a.m. I was always so drunk I could barely walk up those steps outside to get back into the house, I usually crawled.

So how did this happen night after night? Well, a young girl can't sit at a bar all alone without someone offering her a drink. Let's see, there was always someone sending me a drink from across the bar. Yes, that really happens. Or there is someone who wants to introduce themselves and buy me multiple drinks while telling me their entire life story. One night, a man hit the lottery and bought everyone a round. Each one of these would become quite disappointed when I didn't leave with them. As a matter of fact, I would keep a close eye on everyone who talked to me and buy me drinks. I watched to see when they would leave. I never left the bar until they were all gone. I didn't want anybody to know I lived there.

On this one night, I came down to the bar as usual. It was sort of a game for me, and the girls who were working. They would count how many free drinks I ended up getting. Well, this one guy came in already drunk and with an attitude. Of course, when he noticed me, it was on. I had nowhere to hide, and he came right over and started talking to me and buying drinks. During the entire conversation he complained about his wife. It drove me crazy! I wanted to leave but I didn't want to break my own rule. I didn't want this guy to know I lived here. I finally told him to leave me alone. I didn't want any more drinks. The barmaids chimed in as well and told him to sit somewhere else. He was starting to get on everyone's nerves. While someone else had distracted him, I got up and headed for the bathroom.

I felt like it was a nice escape, maybe he would leave while I was in there. Suddenly, I heard a loud crash behind me on the wall. I turned around to see the owner with this same guy pinned to the wall with his feet off the floor. He was screaming at the drunk, saying where do you think you're going? Get out! The owner just physically dragged him outside. I was frozen! What just happened? What almost happened? The owner came back and asked me if I was okay.

"That man tried to follow you into the bathroom," said the owner. "I'll keep watch outside to make sure he doesn't return."

This is exactly what he did, and when it was clear he told me to go back upstairs to my room. I did just that, and this time I didn't crawl up those stairs, I quickly ran up them. I was terrified of the thought of what could have taken place.

After a few days, I did go back to the bar but just to talk to the girls. I had intentions to leave before it got busy. But before I could do that, a man sitting at a table behind me eating his dinner called me the "N" word!

I turned around, looked him in the eye and said, "I'll be right back!"

The barmaid asked if I was ok.

"Yes, I'm just fine!"

I went upstairs to my room and got my knife and put it in the front pocket of my jeans. I draped my shirt around so it could be seen. My knife was huge, there was no mistaking what it was. What did I think I was going to do with this posture I was taking? I had no idea, but I felt like I wasn't about to be punked down by some white guy in a business suit. I walked back into the bar and slowly walked back to my bar stool, staring at this man the whole time. By the time I got back to my seat, he stood up and apologized to me in front of his friends that were with him. I just shook my head and rolled my eyes at him. By the time I sat down and turned my back, they paid their check and left. I had my hand on my knife the whole time. That was the last time I went down to the bar.

I was getting anxious because I still had no job, and I needed to get out of this place. I went downtown as usual and just walked around. I had no plan; it was just something to do now. As I walked, I found myself across from the Greyhound Bus Station. It looked different in the day light. There was a Burger King sign in front of the station. *That's so strange. I didn't realize there was a restaurant in the bus station.* I crossed the street and went inside to fill out an application.

I completed a lengthy application. The manager arrived just as I finished it. As he reviewed it, he appeared to be puzzled.

"Why are you applying for this job?" he said. "You're overqualified. You should be working in a hospital."

"I'm new to the city, sir, with no car and I need to move." I explained. I need money now!"

He showed me compassion and hired me on the spot.

So just like that I had a job and some hope. I worked 3–4 days a week. I was allowed to eat one meal per day, and I was taught to do everything: clean, stock, cook, and run the register.

I went back to the hotel to tell my girlfriends working at the bar that I had a job. They were excited for me. Christmas was fast approaching, and I needed to find a cheap place to live that was close to the bus station. I searched the paper and found a place downtown that was like the situation I was in now. A hotel bar with rooms to rent, and it was much cheaper with weekly rent. I called to see if they still had rooms available to rent, and they did. They were somewhere on 9th street. The next day was Saturday, and I didn't have to work, so I set this as my moving day.

I packed up my things and realized I had accumulated quite a bit of stuff. I had a box, and a few bags. I couldn't carry all of this on the bus at one time, so I realized I would have to make a few trips. No one at the hotel was able to give me a ride, so it had to be the bus. I got up early, said my goodbyes and thanks to everyone, grabbed what I could carry, and caught the bus downtown. I would never see The Evergreen Hotel again. I heard that there was a fire, and then it was demolished in 2011.

Once downtown I walked to 9th Street to the address. The building was nondescript. I almost walked past it. There was no sign, just the address number. I rang the bell, and I believe I was buzzed in. It was the strangest building. I walked into a long narrow hallway with a man at a tall desk almost like a podium, just sitting there. A middle-aged white man stood behind it with no expression on his face. There was no greeting from him, he just stared at me. I introduced myself and said we spoke yesterday about the room. He affirmed this and showed me the room on the second floor. It was small with a twin bed, a dresser, maybe a closet, and one window that faced the wall of another building. It did look clean, so I said I'd take it. I paid him and put my things on the bed. I told him I would be making a couple more trips to get the rest of my things. Then I left for the bus.

I ended up taking two more trips downtown. On the last trip, I was frozen and tired. I got buzzed back into the building and as I entered, I saw the strangest thing that made me stop in my tracks. The door on my left swung open; I didn't even notice this door before. A young girl in a white robe walked through, and we locked eyes for what seemed to be an eternity. She looked like she was my age. She had a pretty face, but she had a strange, sad expression on her face. I looked behind her through the door, just to see people in a bar facing a stage. I was looking at the back of the stage where a naked woman was on a swing. Then the door shut closed. The young girl just turned and walked up the stairs. I said nothing, but my heart was racing. I went up to my room, closed the door and panicked.

I can't stay here. Now what am I going to do!

I ran back down to the guy at the desk.

"You know, I change my mind about the room, can I get my money back?"

"Yes," he said. "I figured you would ask me that."

"Sir, do you know of any other hotels with rooms to rent?"

"Yes, I think you would be more comfortable at The Ellis Hotel on Centre Avenue."

I had no idea where Centre Avenue was. I asked for a phone number so I could see if they had anything available. To my surprise, this man picked up the phone and called himself, spoke to someone briefly and hung up. "Yes, they have rooms available." He gave me directions as to how to get there, and he gave me my money back, and he let me hold the key since I obviously had to start this journey all over again, but this time walking. It took me two struggling trips this time. I just didn't have the energy for a third.

Ellis

The Ellis was a grand hotel in Pittsburgh's Hill District, earning a listing in *The Green Book*. *The Green Book* was a directory for Black travelers to find welcoming and safe places to receive services. The Ellis Hotel was also a part of Pittsburgh's jazz culture, hosting artists such as Ella Fitzgerald, Duke Ellington, Miles Davis, Ray Charles, and many other famous artists.

As I approached The Ellis Hotel, I could see people dining through the large, framed window. Then the main doors to the building and another door further down that led into the bar. It was an old building that had the appearance of once being great and beautiful. I walked through the main doors, noticing a lot of activity of people coming and going from the restaurant to my right. I stood in a large foyer that had the markings of detailed architecture. To my left was a front desk area enclosed with glass like a booth with a door at the other end. Two black women stood looking at me as I entered. One greeted me with a warm, beautiful smile.

"Welcome to The Ellis Hotel. How can I help you?"

The other woman was not smiling and did not greet me but instead she looked at me as if to say, "who are you?" I directed my attention to the nicer of the two women and explained that the recent phone call she received was about me and the need for a room. She asked me how I found the other hotel. I explained it to her and that I quickly realized that I didn't want to be there. She agreed and told me about the rates per week, and I paid her. The other woman showed me the room.

As we ascended the stairs to the second floor, this woman roughly briefed me on all the rules of the hotel. Her tone with me was sharp, but I was too tired to act like I was going to protest. I thanked her and said I had to get the rest of my belongings.

When I finally returned, I took a look around my room. I checked under the bed. I wanted to see if it was dirty or if anything was under there. The bed coverings seemed clean but just old. I had a dresser and a sink. What a plus to having running water in my room, but the bathroom was a large community bathroom down the hall with a tub, sinks and toilets. I had a window that looked out from the side of the building, so I could see most of the activity on the street. I realized my room was right over the bar. Across the hall from my room was a fancy-enclosed phone booth. It looked like something from the movies. I checked it out and wrote down the number. I hadn't reached out to any of my family members or friends yet to let them know I was alive and well. Now I have a number to give them to contact me. I finally laid down on top of the covers and passed out.

The next day I got up early to take full inventory of what and who was around me. My room was down the hall from the top of the stairs. This building was very large, and it didn't appear that way from the outside. I looked around my room again and tried to figure out what I needed. I needed cleaning supplies, a few more items of clothes, and shoes. I didn't have much money, but I did have my Sears credit card that I was holding on to for any emergency. I applied for it when I was in Philadelphia. I had no idea where the Sears department store was located in the city. I didn't notice any downtown, so I needed to do some investigating.

I went downstairs to talk to the ladies I met yesterday to see if they could help me. Sure enough, I was given directions to Sears, but I needed to take the bus to a different part of town on the North side. I went back upstairs to get what I needed for the trip and made a list of what I needed. When I got up the stairs, I noticed a young man mopping the floor. I asked him how often he did this, and he said every day. I asked if he could mop out my room really quick and get under the bed really good. He said, yes ma'am. Even though he gave me a little bit of a skeptical look, he did as I asked. I didn't have a tip for him, so I just gave him a big smile and thank you. He probably thought I was around his age. He smiled back and seemed to be satisfied with that. As I was leaving, I noticed the room next to me had a big pad lock on the door. I also heard a TV and smelled food.

Hmm. I don't think any of that is in agreement with the rule book I was blasted with the night before. Oh well. Not my business.

I caught the bus and found my way with no problem. Seeing another part of town was exciting, a new adventure. Being in Sears brought back amazing memories of my mom and I shopping on the weekends. As strange as it may sound, I felt like I was back in the land of the living. The word grateful doesn't even cut it.

Overwhelmed, I didn't know what to look at first. I had to remember the mission. The first thing I found was a metal shopping cart. Not the type in the grocery store but the small fold up kind people use to carry things when they're walking.

This will be very useful to me since I travel on the bus, and I expect to buy some things I can't carry in my hands.

I purchased a better coat, shoes, jeans and a few shirts. Then I saw a 13-inch black and white TV on sale. Perfect! I got some ear plugs so I could listen without anyone else hearing it. I picked up the other things on my list and was about to leave when I noticed a cafeteria within the store. I entered it and asked the cashier if this was a part of Sears and if I could buy food with my credit card. When she said yes, I almost fell over. *Thank you, Jesus!*

Chapter Four: Hotel Angels

I ordered a big lunch and relaxed.

When I returned to The Ellis, I passed the two ladies at the booth. The pleasant one asked how my trip was, and the other said nothing, just stared. I had everything neatly packed in my cart. As I approached the stairs, I could still feel the eyes of the one lady on me. I thought, I hope she can't see this box with the TV in it. I hurried up the stairs and got in my room. I put all my things away and set up my TV. It was wonderful! Then there was a knock at my door. It was the non-smiling desk clerk. She said the manager wanted to speak to me in his office.

I thought to myself, *What manager?! I didn't know there was a manager.*

I followed her down to his office, and believe me, I had an attitude all over me when I entered. This was a large black man, who for all intents and purposes, was quite intimidating. I couldn't have cared less. I just ran away from a "beast," so let's see what this one is all about!

He read me the riot act. He said I had a TV, and that wasn't allowed, he said I was too young to be living there. He said he didn't want any prostitutes living in his building. I let him have his podium but then it was my turn. First off, I'm no prostitute! I have a job! The phone outside my room rings all night and they're men calling for women and women answer the phone. Yes, I have a TV, and I'm not getting rid of it! There is someone living next door to me with a pad lock on their door, with a TV and cooking food. Oh, and let me show you my driver's license right now so you know my age. I had my driver's license on me, and I showed it to him.

"You're about to turn 21!" he said. He was shocked! Suddenly, he got this big greasy smile on his face. "You're a feisty one!" He started to laugh. "Okay, I just don't want any trouble out of you!" he said.

I replied, "You won't get any!" I started back up the steps to my room, not looking happy on purpose. When I passed the booth, my pleasant friend looked sad. She probably thought I was being kicked out. The other lady had her usual look. I said nothing to either of them and continued up to my room.

The next morning, I was getting ready to go to work. To my surprise, I received a good morning from both ladies. I was speechless! I had to remember to close my mouth and smile.

Where did that come from?

The days continued, and I worked and saved my money.

I started to recognize more of the people around me in my little community at the hotel. There was an elderly gentleman who lived directly across from me.

He was shy at first, but he started having short conversations with me until one day he started asking me to sew his buttons on his shirts and mending other clothes.

The man next door was like a ghost. I never saw him until one day I was going into my room, and he was coming out of his. When the door opened, I got a glimpse of everything in his room. Just like I thought. A TV, a boom box, and a hot plate and it was decorated. I tried not to stare too long because he was staring at me. It was a brief moment, but when I returned my gaze to him, he nodded and walked away, no words. It was a little creepy, but I was glad he didn't say anything. I continued to see the young boy mopping the floor, and I would catch him before he started so he could mop my floor with clean water. He didn't smile at me the way he did the first time he just said yes ma'am and did what I asked.

Even the grouchy lady at the desk was nice. She said good morning every morning now, and she would give me extra sheets when I asked for them. That was also against the rules. We were only supposed to get sheets once a week, but I asked for them every other day.

Even looking out my window was entertainment. I learned a lot. For example, during the day it was a quiet and peaceful neighborhood. Everyone is going about their business with no problems. At night though, it was a different story. Women of the night came out and came through the doors of this building. They answered the phone outside of my room all the time. The drug dealers were lined up on the street outside and the traffic never stopped. They were fascinating to observe. I learned new slang by listening to them all night. I had no idea what "roll call" meant or "Five 0," but I caught on while watching their behavior associated with the slang. I saw people get beaten up, and I heard about a stabbing right at the front door of the building. I was in a dangerous place, surrounded by some dangerous people, but also surrounded by God's protection. I wasn't even scared.

There were many good people there as well—God's Angels, I call them. One of them was the cook in the restaurant who would cook my Ramen Noodles for me every night and didn't charge me anything. There was also a young man once who saw me talking to the cook and stopped me and said he wanted to have lunch with me. I looked at him funny because I didn't know him or where he came from. I looked at the cook, and he gave me this nod of approval. So, I sat down with this guy who didn't look much older than me. He said order whatever you want, my treat. I got nervous and started to get up. I didn't want to know what the price of this meal was going to be, but he assured me he wanted nothing in return. So, with that I sat back down and had a wonderful baked chicken dinner and conversation. When the meal was over, he said goodbye and left. I never saw the young man again.

I lived in The Ellis through Christmas and New Year's, turned 21 and watched winter turn into spring. I was getting comfortable there. I felt like I could plan for a better job now that I was getting more familiar with the city. I found a nursing agency in the paper that could do the work of finding my next job. I was really excited about the future.

Chapter Five

"How long am I to feel anxious in my soul, with grief in my heart all the day? How long will my enemy be exalted over me?" Psalm 13:2

Letter Attacks

I returned from work one afternoon, and my friends in the booth called me over and said I had mail. I was happy, maybe it was my mom or one of my friends. I was so excited I didn't want to look at it until I got up to my room. I sat on the bed, got comfortable and looked at the envelope. My heart started to race, and I felt faint. It was from Philadelphia, it was from Mr. Man. I was shaking. I opened the letter and read it. He apologized. He wanted me to come back home. He promised everything would be better. He said he couldn't eat or sleep without me.

What kind of nonsense is this! How did he know where I was?

Then I remembered my wonderful time at Sears. I didn't think to change the billing address with them. He must have seen the charges here in Pittsburgh.

But to this day, I don't know how he got the actual address. No matter, I now know my comfort was just an illusion; it was time to find a new place to live and fast. I tore up the letter and tried to come up with a new game plan.

I was contacted by the nursing agency, and they found a job for me at a nursing home in East Liberty. It was along the bus route, so I took it. They had to check my credentials, so I had little time to see if I could find a cheap apartment. I looked all over, but it was either too expensive or too far from the bus route. Then I saw an ad in the paper for a 3rd floor apartment in Garfield.

Oh, my goodness, that's close to where the job is located.

When I contacted the man renting the apartment, I scheduled a time to meet him and see it. The rent was only $150. I couldn't believe it. How could the rent be so cheap? I took $50 with me just in case I liked it, and he would hold it for me. A little trick I learned along the way. The apartment was cute as a button. It needed cleaning and some paint but to me it was paradise. I asked him why the rent was so cheap. He said he bought the property with a government loan, and a stipulation was that the rent had to be low until after he owned the property for a year then he could raise the rent. Sounded good to me! It was in my favor, and I was so happy! I couldn't wait to start putting some sweat equity into it and making it my own. I gave him the $50 to hold the apartment, and the deal was sealed. I signed the lease, and it was done.

I went back to The Ellis Hotel and told my friends the good news. They were happy for me but sad too. We really were a little family there. I was going to miss them. This time when I moved, I didn't have to take the bus. I learned what Jitneys were and called one. I rode to my new home in style. Unfortunately, I never went back to visit those ladies. The Ellis Hotel suffered many hard times and had a fire in 1995, it was finally demolished in 2002. In its place stands a brand-new YMCA.

I started my new job and got settled into my new apartment. I cleaned, painted and decorated. It was now comfortable.

Comfortable, what a deceiving word that can be sometimes.

I worked hard to get this little place in shape. I scrubbed everything with bleach, with Lysol, with anything that would kill whatever I couldn't see. I had a dresser but no bed, a couch sitting on cinder blocks because it didn't have legs and a refrigerator that I didn't dare open because I knew it was rotten! I used that Sears credit card a lot to get it all clean and livable. I purchased a bed and used mattress from a secondhand store down the street. They were nice enough to help me walk it back up the hill to my apartment. I asked my neighbor if he knew anyone that would get rid of the fridge. He came up to look at it and muscled it out of the small kitchen over to the window. Down below my window was a wooded hillside. Before I could say anything, he picked up one end and pushed it through the window, down into the trees below.

I was stunned—but I just smiled and said, "Thank you."

He smiled back. "No problem."

He turned around and went back down to his apartment.

As for the sofa, I vacuumed it, scrubbed it, and sprayed so much Lysol on it until it was damp. I still couldn't fix my mind to sit on it. Looking at it made me itch. I went out and bought the prettiest sofa cover I could find and some blankets to cover it. Finally, I was satisfied. I still needed a fridge. I asked around, and I was advised to go to the Salvation Army. I took the bus to the Southside and walked into this huge Salvation Army. It had furniture, clothes and a refrigerator! I couldn't believe it! It was one of those old-fashioned kinds that was short and had rounded edges. It would fit perfectly in the space in the kitchen. The price was perfect too, $50. I purchased it immediately. Then my heart sank.

How am I going to get this home and up to the third floor?

First, I had to get it back to East Liberty. I had a habit of keeping the phone numbers of the Jitney's I used before. So, I went to the payphone and started calling until I found someone with a station wagon. I offered a big tip to make sure they would really come get me, and an hour later they showed up. The fridge fit in the vehicle perfectly. We didn't talk much on the ride because now I had to figure out how to get this upstairs. Once we arrived in front of the house, I had it all figured out. Another habit I had was keeping a case of beer in my kitchen. I really didn't drink much beer, so sometimes I would have more than one case sitting around. The beer distributor was right across the street. Every pay day, I would just buy a case of beer. Living alone with no help, I learned quickly this was a great bartering tool. Anytime someone helped me with a big favor they got a six pack of beer, and I sent them on their way. So, this was the plan.

The Jitney driver asked, "How are you going to get this inside. Do you have help?"

"Yes." Then I yelled up at my neighbors' open window. His wife looked out. "Could your husband help my driver get this fridge up to my apartment?"

She said let me get him. Her husband, the same guy who pushed my old fridge out the window, thought I was crazy, as did the driver. I told them both they would get a six pack of beer, and I reminded the driver that he was getting a substantial tip. I do believe the mention of receiving free beer was really all it took for them to work so hard. In no time, the refrigerator was in its place in my kitchen, working like a charm. I had all the essentials needed to be comfortable.

There's that word again. I was so comfortable I was starting to forget how the Lord brought me through. I didn't understand the favor I was receiving was from Him. Instead, I just wanted to forget all the previous pain.

I looked around my cute little place and realized I was lonely. I started making friends, some good, most not so good. I was hanging out with guys that were not worth my time, but they were my drinking buddies. Yes, I started drinking again, bar hopping. Seeing and experiencing all sorts of crazy things. *I was so lost so fast!* I wasn't looking for a church. I wasn't reading a Bible. I felt I was too far gone. Why would God want anything to do with me now? I had no direction and didn't see much of a future for myself except for what I was doing. All I knew was I wanted to be here. I didn't want to go home. This was my home now. I didn't want to run anymore. I just felt so tired and defeated.

I came home from work one evening and grabbed the mail and went upstairs. I sat down and there was another letter from Philadelphia. I started to tremble; my heart was racing. It was another letter from him! *How does he keep finding me?* He said this was enough and it was time to come home. He said he would forgive me for whatever I was doing and everything would be alright—I just needed to come home.

What is he talking about? That was not my home! This is my home!

He was sterner in this letter than the last. At the end of the letter, he gave a warning for whatever guy he thought I might be seeing: "Watch her. She will do the same to you."

I couldn't believe this was happening again. My nerves were rattled. I think he's stalking me! The last letter was a month ago. I wasn't sure what to do. The few friends I talked to about it said not to worry.

"He's just trying to scare you."

Well, he's doing a great job at that. I was shaken up for days. I couldn't sleep, and I drank even more. I felt that old fear building back up, and I didn't want it!

Chapter Six

"Behold, I am doing a new thing; now it springs forth, do you not perceive it? I will make a way in the wilderness and rivers in the desert." Isaiah 43:19

Angel from my Past: God's Protection in my Wilderness

Two weeks went by, and I started to relax. Maybe he was just bluffing. He's still trying to control me but from a distance. When I came home and grabbed the mail, there was another letter. I felt numb, cold and the tears began to flow. No, no, no! Not again! I started pacing the floor and opened the letter. It was threatening this time.

"I've had enough; I'm coming to get you! And I'm bringing my boys with me!"

Of all the nasty things he said in the letter, this was the only part that stood out.

He's coming, and he's not alone.

I stared at the letter with trembling hands. I thought of his friends. They're as scary as he is, but would they really follow him? It took a minute, but then I realized he was bringing them in case I had my own crew who would fight for me. Yeah right. I was all alone, or so I thought.

I was starting to lose my mind.

It only takes about 5-6 hours to drive here from Philly. What time is it? Wait, what if he's already here?

I ran to the windows looking around. I closed all the blinds.

I must leave now! I'll throw some things in a bag. I don't have much in the bank, but I will close out the account and buy a bus ticket. Where am I going?

I started to cry.

I don't know where I'm going!

I was making my way to the bedroom to grab a bag when the phone rang.

Who could that be? Is it him? How did he get my number?

I just stood there staring at the phone as it rang.

Pick up the phone, Trudy.

I ran and picked up the phone, but I didn't say anything. A woman's voice said, "Trudy? Are you there?"

I felt like I was holding my breath for a very long time. "Yes, yes, I'm here!"

It was my girlfriend, Murphy.

"You were on my mind all day; I had to call you," she exclaimed. "Are you alright?"

I started crying, "No I'm not alright."

I still clutched the threatening letter in my hand as I told her what was going on. I read the letters to her so she could understand my fear. But she was so calm. She spoke to me so softly.

"Now Trudy, this is what you're going to do. You're going to mail those letters to me, ok? Do you have any information about him?"

"I have his social security number since I did the taxes! I also have our last address and his mother's address."

"Okay, that's good, but isn't he driving your car?" she reminded me.

"Oh, my goodness! I almost forgot!" I yelled.

I gave her the make, model, and license plate number. I may have even given her the VIN number. I kept some paperwork from my car. I did so much work on it. I literally purchased it out of a junk yard and restored it. It was a 1973 Camaro. It was all in my name, not his, and he's driving it like it belongs to him!

She took all the information, and I promised to mail her the letters.

Then Murphy said, "Relax, take a deep breath. He's not coming to Pittsburgh. I have all I need."

"But I was about to pack and run!" I said desperately.

"Don't you like Pittsburgh?"

"Yes."

"Then stay in Pittsburgh. You don't have to worry about him. He's not going anywhere, and you will never see him again."

What is she saying to me? How can she know this?

Her voice was so reassuring, so confident that I trusted what she was saying. I began to calm down a little.

I know her husband is in law enforcement, and she may be asking him for assistance. That must be why she asked me for all the information. But, God, you told her to call me today! You told her I needed help! I'm not supposed to run anymore.

That was the last time I spoke to my dear friend. I never got another letter. Over the years I have lost my friend's phone number and address, but I will never forget that day.

Epilogue

I continued to live in Pittsburgh, but it took a long time to let go of the fear. I always looked over my shoulder. After I was married and started having children, I was still nervous to take them anywhere alone. I let the fear grip me for years. What would I do if I saw him, and I was alone with my children? How would I protect them?

The years went by with all life's ups and downs, and I still had not acknowledged God for how He brought me through. How He protected me from my enemies. I still couldn't see; I was blinded. I wasn't trusting in Him, and I continued to feel defeated. I walked away from God so many times, I was sure He didn't want anything to do with me. But that was exactly what the enemy, Satan, wanted me to think. He wanted me to forget the details of God's goodness in my life. His protection, His grace and mercy! He kept me! I lived many years being bitter, angry and confused. To others, it appeared as though I had everything under control, but on the inside and behind closed doors, everything was wrong.

My health was starting to act up, my family was acting up, and my hope was taking a nosedive! That's when God started speaking to me again. The Holy Spirit was giving me directions, like He did so long ago. I thought I was losing my mind.

Whose voice am I hearing? It wasn't mine because I would have done these things a long time ago if I had thought of them. It wasn't the Devil because what I am to do will benefit my health. It must be God, so I'll listen and respond.

My directions were to get my health in order. Lose weight, exercise, eat right, or I'm not going to make it. My God, I was shaking, crying, but I got up! I did what I was told. I became healthier and felt stronger. No more diabetes, no more hypertension, and no more sleep apnea. I looked and felt younger. It was hard to believe. I told everyone how I did it, and God gave me the strength to do it. That's when I usually lost folks in the conversation, but it didn't stop me. I didn't do this on my own. My birthday was coming up and my husband and I went out to celebrate. I was wearing clothing that I could never have worn a year ago. I decided to visit my family in Florida and continue celebrating. I had a great time and when I returned, the city was shutting down for COVID-19. Then I remembered my directions from the Holy Spirit.

As the pandemic roared through the country and the world, I realized I had most of the chronic conditions that would have made me high risk for contracting COVID. If I had not listened to the word of the Lord, I may not have survived. I told a friend I didn't know why God showed me such favor. You see, up to this point, I still had not truly thanked God for what He had done in my life. I had not gotten on my knees to repent for not trusting Him. Before the year was out more things began to crash all around me in my life concerning my family. I was devastated, confused, and that fear came rushing back. Every bad decision I ever made was based on fear. On top of all that I was now dealing with my past. It came back to visit me.

It came back to haunt me, to crush me and it almost succeeded. I found out that my oppressor was dead. You may think that my first reaction was to celebrate. But I didn't. I was angry! I was enraged!

Look what you did to me! Look what you took from me! I'll never get it back! I wanted to be the one who killed you! I wanted to be the one who made you suffer! Now you're just dead. And I still feel your pain!

I was losing my mind. I couldn't sleep. I couldn't concentrate. I cried for anything and everything and nothing. My mood swings were intolerable. I had my annual PCP appointment and cried all through it. She's never seen me this way. She was ready to write a prescription for antidepressants. That scared me. I wasn't ready for that yet, or was I? I told my doctor I would think about it. She suggested a therapist and entered a referral for me. Nothing came of it though; all we did was play phone tag, and eventually I gave up.

In a way I was relieved, I didn't want to talk to a stranger. I decided to call one of my sisters and explain my feelings to her. For weeks I rambled on to her about things. I cried, I was angry, I was depressed, she heard it all. I must have sounded crazy. I was to the point where I just wanted to give up. I needed a break. I contemplated checking into the nearest behavior health hospital. Maybe it was time to be medicated. Just walk away from the world for a minute. But I kept hearing that voice: *You won't be able to hear me.*

I was frightened. I called my sister. God bless her, she's been listening to me revolve around the same subject for a while now, but on this day her frustration started to show a little.

While we were talking on the phone, she interrupted me by saying, "Trudy, you have to pray!"

All kinds of attitude were wrapped up in that statement, and I felt it! There was a moment of silence on the phone. Now I have an attitude.

What does she think I'm doing? I thought to myself.

She came back on the line and the tone of her voice was totally different, calm and soothing.

"Trudy, just talk to Him."

Epilogue

Those few words felt like a ton of bricks just fell on me! The tears started to flow but I tried to hide it. She was right. I wasn't praying at all.

With my best voice I told my sister, "I will. Thank you. I'll talk to you later."

All this time it was my sister, who had been ministering to me, praying for me, reading me scriptures, not me. She even told me how heavy my situation was on her. My God. When I got off the phone, I ran to my bedroom and shut the door. Down to my knees I fell, and I called on Jesus.

Lord forgive me! Please come back to me. I will never leave you again. I can't do any of this life without you. Wash me clean with your blood, Lord, please! I want to hear your voice again!

I couldn't cry another tear; a calm came over me as I sat on the floor. I thanked God for keeping this stubborn, foolish woman all these years.

Then the Lord said, "I never left you."

That was the day I rededicated my life to God. Thank you, Jesus! I've been holding on to the hem of His garment ever since. I will never let Him go! As for all those circumstances that were weighing me down, I gave them to Jesus. I let Him take on that burden, it was too heavy for me. I stopped crying over things and people I can't change. I'm learning to be more like Jesus and get out of God's way.

God has His own way and timing for everything, and it's perfect! My testimony proves that. He let me go through situations in my life, just to show me He was the only one who could get me out. That way He gets all the glory, and I reap the benefits of His grace and mercy. He placed people, I call them Angels, along the way to protect and guide me. All of them may not have had a relationship with God, but they listened to Him concerning me.

My story is not unique, not special in any way. Unfortunately, there are many women who have suffered much worse, and many did not survive to tell their stories. But this is more than just a story, it's my testimony. I testify to the goodness of God! I testify to His gift of life and salvation through Jesus Christ! Unlike a story that must end, a testimony of God's grace and mercy continues to mark new beginnings.

Afterword

"Behold, I stand at the door and knock; if anyone hears My voice and opens the door, I will come in to him and will dine with him, and he with Me."
Revelation 3:20

Are you weighed down by the burdens of this life? Is anxiety and fear the driving force in your decision making? Have you gone numb to your condition and the condition of this world? Do you want to feel life in a way you have never felt before? Do you want to know a true love that will last for all eternity?

Jesus came to this world as a human child, helpless and poor to save humanity. He didn't look like a king, a ruler, a conqueror, or all mighty, but that is exactly who He was then, and who He is now. He's not hanging on a tree anymore and His tomb is still empty. Glory to God! He suffered and died. He was buried and rose again, conquering death and guaranteeing eternal life. Why? Because He loves you. You have only to accept this gift and it's yours. Jesus will give you life and show you love that you have never experienced. He cares for you, so He'll take your burdens so that you can

Afterword

be free. He'll give you peace and joy beyond anything you can possibly imagine.

For those of you who were like me, who keep walking away from God, for those who are running and avoiding the call of God—there is no where you can run or hide that God isn't already there. We can't live this life without Him. We can't do it alone. Stop running, because you know you're tired, you're exhausted. Just look up, His hand is already reaching out to you. Trust Him. Just talk to Him.

If you are ready to accept this precious gift that comes with a price tag that none of us could afford, then pray these words to:

Dear Heavenly Father,

I confess my sins and ask for Your forgiveness. I believe that Your Son, Jesus was born of a virgin, died on the cross and rose on the third day to conquer death and give me life eternal. Jesus, I invite You into my heart as my Lord and Savior. Take complete control of my life and help me to walk in Your footsteps daily by the power of the Holy Spirit. Thank You, Lord, for saving me and answering my prayer.

In Jesus's name, Amen.

"If you confess with your mouth, 'Jesus is Lord,' and believe in your heart that God raised Him from the

Afterword

dead, you will be saved. For everyone that calls on the name of the Lord will be saved." Romans 10:9, 13

If you prayed that prayer sincerely, the Angels in heaven are rejoicing! You are a child of the King!

So, what's next?

Find a Bible that is easy for you to read and start reading every day. This is God's love letter to you. Jesus speaks directly to you with love, promises and everything you need to know to live this life. Remember, He walked this earth like us, so He knows your struggles.

Talk to the Lord. Pray every day. Build the relationship you have been longing for. Talk to Him. Get to know Him. Fall in love with your Lord and Savior, your friend.

Find a body of Christ, a church. We are instructed to worship and join in fellowship with other Believers. We weren't meant to walk this walk alone. The House of God should teach from God's Word, the Bible. The foundation of their belief should be in God the Father, God the Son (Jesus), and God the Holy Spirit. They should give instructions on serving, discipleship, salvation through Jesus Christ, Baptism in the Spirit and Baptism in water.

Last, but certainly not least, tell someone about Jesus! Share your testimony of His grace and mercy in your life. May the all mighty God bless and keep you, in Jesus's name, Amen.

"Give thanks to the Lord, for He is good, for His mercy is everlasting. The redeemed of the Lord shall say so, those whom He redeemed from the hand of the enemy and gathered from the lands, from the east and from the west, from the north and from the south." Psalm 107:1-3

Acknowledgements

To my husband, Howard, and children, Trenita and Alexis. Thank you for your love and encouragement.

To my extended family, sisters, brother, nieces and nephews. Thank you for your love and prayers.

To my dear friends and colleagues, thank you for your love and support.

To my Pastor, Michael Anthony Day, and First Lady Pastor, Ambor Day. I don't have enough words to express my gratefulness to you for your leadership, support and prayers.

To my spiritual family at Legacy International Worship Center, you know how much I love you all! Thank you for your love and prayers.

About the Author

Trudy Finney was born in Long Island, New York and raised in Burlington, New Jersey by her parents, Alberta, a native of Nicaragua, and Edward, a Navy veteran from Florence, New Jersey. As a young child, she lived close to her grandparents, Elmer and Vera Matthews. She was also surrounded by her uncle Arthur and aunt Christine and their children, Craig, Kelvin, Kent and Brenda. They were more like siblings than first cousins.

She arrived in Pittsburgh, Pennsylvania at the age of twenty. This is where she received her education and started her career. She has been living in this beautiful city for forty years now. She has lived there longer than she lived at home, so she is officially a Pittsburgher.

She accepted Jesus as her Lord and Savior at the age of thirteen and was baptized at the age of fourteen. At that time, she was attending First Christian Assembly in Burlington, New Jersey with Reverend Samuel Montagano. After living in Pittsburgh for a few years, she attended the Pentecostal Temple Church with then Bishop Loran Mann and First Lady, now Pastor

Barbara Mann, where their first born was dedicated. In 2021, she rededicated her life to Christ, and the Lord brought her to her current church home. In 2023, she became a member of and was baptized at Legacy International Worship Center with Pastor Michael Anthony Day and First Lady Pastor Amber Day. Her spiritual family!

The Lord chose and blessed her with a career in nursing that spanned 42 years. In that time, she met many wonderful people from all walks of life, whom the Lord placed in her path, to share His love and care. During the last 27 years of her career, she proudly served the nation's finest, the Veterans, at the Pittsburgh VA Healthcare System, from where she recently retired.

She attended the Community College of Allegheny County, Allegheny Campus, and received an Associate Degree in Nursing. She then attended Carlow University and received both her bachelor's and master's degrees in nursing, obtaining Board Certification as a Family Nurse Practitioner.

The Lord has shown her favor with being married to her loving husband of 35 years, Howard. They were blessed with two beautiful daughters, Trenita and Alexis. She loves to spend time with her family and cuddling their gorgeous pitbull, Snowball. Now that she is retired, she has more time to travel with her siblings. She is the youngest of eight children. She has five sisters and one living brother, and when they are all together, they are so blessed. Alvin, Lorraine, Joyce, Edith, Lydia and Alberta, she loves them all so much! The oldest, her big brother, who was ever present in her life, Viques, passed away in 2009.

With the time the Lord has so graciously given her, she can continue her love for reading, writing, art, crocheting, and most importantly, serving within the body of Christ. She is a woman of God, wife, mother and friend with a new full-time position, working for God!

Bibliography

Amanda Ryczek and Dianne Lemon. "Ellis Hotel." *Hill District*
> *Digital History.* Accessed April 24, 2025. https://hillhistory.org.

Benjamin Franklin Bridge. *Wikipedia.* Accessed April 24, 2025.
> https://en.wikipedia.org/wiki/Benjamin_Franklin_Bridge.

Burger King. Accessed April 24, 2025. https://www.bk.com.
> (Referenced on page 21.)

The Evergreen Hotel. *The Odd, Mysterious & Fascinating History*
> *of Pittsburgh.* Facebook, 2018. https://www.facebook.com.

Florida Department of Corrections. "Historical Timeline: 1980–1986." Accessed April 24, 2025. https://fdc-media.ccplatform.net/historical-archive/1980-1986.html. (Referenced on page 15.)

The Green Book. *Encyclopedia Britannica.* Accessed April 24, 2025. https://www.britannica.com/topic/The-Green-Book-travel-guide.

Greyhound Bus. Accessed April 24, 2025.
> https://www.greyhound.com. (Referenced on pages 5 and 13.)

Pittsburgh Holiday Parade. *Wikipedia.* Accessed April 24,

2025. https://en.wikipedia.org/wiki/Celebrate_the_Season_Parade. (Referenced on page 18.)

Psycho. *Wikipedia*. Accessed April 24, 2025. https://en.wikipedia.org/wiki/Psycho. (Referenced on page 18.)

INDEX

alone, iii, 20, 55, 56, 75, 79, 83, 90, 91
anguish, 17
antidepressants, 85
Art Institute, 1
Babcock Blvd, 48
Baptism, 91
Benjamin Franklin Bridge, 7, 99
Burger King, 58, 99
Camden, 9
confusion, 18
content, 3
courage, 19
COVID-19, 84
cruelty, 18
decision, 2, 17, 85, 89
deliverance, iii
dementia, 1
desolation, iii
disobedience, 19
distractions, 5, 10
duffle bag, 24
Duke Ellington, 62
East Liberty, 72, 75
Ella Fitzgerald, 62
Evergreen Hotel, 59
faith, ii, iii
fear, 1, 6, 13, 17, 19, 20, 21, 78, 81, 83, 85, 89
fears, iii
forgiveness, 23, 90
Franklin Square, 13
free, 3
goal, 5
God the Father, 7, 91
God the Holy Spirit, 91
God the Son, 91
graphic designer, 1
green sheet, 41, 48
Greyhound Bus Station, 58
Gyros, 52
hoagies, 48, 49, 51
Holiday Parade, 45, 99
Holy Spirit, 23
hoodie, 12
identity, 17
intimate, iii
Jitney's, 38, 75
Legacy International Worship Center, ii, 93
local employment agency, 2
loneliness, iii
Lysol, 73, 74
medicated, 86
micromanaged, 6
Miles Davis, 62
mood swings, 85
murder, 18
nurse, 1, 3
nursing facility, 3
oppressor, 17, 85

pack, 23, 24, 75, 76, 81
pain, iii, 76, 85
pandemic, 84
PCP, 85
permission, 3
phone book, 41
pray, 5, 13, 86, 90
prison, 18, 36, 38
protect, 5, 17, 83, 88
Psycho, 44
purpose, 3
Ramen Noodles, 69
Ray Charles, 62
Salvation Army, 74
Sears, 64, 65, 71, 73
shame, i, 8, 19
stalking, 77
strength, ii
struggles, iii, 91
suicide, 18
survive, 17
terror, 11

Thanksgiving, 26, 27, 28, 29, 30, 40
The Benjamin Franklin Bridge, 13
The Ellis Hotel, 61, 62, 73
The Green Book, 61, 99
therapist, 85
threats, 6, 7, 17
thuggish, 12
torment, 17, 19
transformation, iii
transforms, iii
trapped, 18
trial, i
value, 3
victory, i
violent, 18
voice of God, 23
works, 3
worthless, 19
YMCA, 73

www.ingramcontent.com/pod-product-compliance
Lightning Source LLC
Chambersburg PA
CBHW032055150426
43194CB00006B/537